Publishing Services provided by Stanton Publishing House

ISBN-13: 9781079591996 (KDP Amazon)

ISBN-13: 9781987098006 (Barnes & Nobles)

Library of Congress Number: 2019914126

Printed in the United States of America

DISCLAIMER:

This memoir was written at a time where I was really angry, really frustrated, really depressed, and just in desperate need to get my story out. There are moments where the language use is not conducive to my being a daughter of Fisk University, a woman of Sigma Gamma Rho Sorority, Incorporated, and a licensed professional counselor with the State of Illinois. There are also moments where the feelings expressed about certain people, places, and things could be perceived as hate or extreme pessimism. As such I ask two things of the reader(s) of this memoir:

1. Please forgive the language and feel free to screen this reading for any female under the age of 18

2. Please forgive the use of language towards my friends and family. These were my feelings in the moment; they do not, in any way, reflect my current sentiments.

Crossroads

KAWANA WILLIAMS

CROSSROADS

PROLOGUE

Imagine waking up on Monday morning, preparing for your day.

Your family has already left home: for school, for work, or for

whatever it is they do during the day. You're standing in the

kitchen, enjoying your coffee, and filtering through your mental

"To Do List." The sun is shining; your belly is full from breakfast

and "have a nice day" salutations. A smile comes across your face,

knowing that today is going to be a wonderful day. Time passes,

and a knock comes at your door. You saunter to the door,

continuing to smile at the mere thought of how good your day will

be. You open your front door, greeted by two police officers who

swiftly and immediately remove their hats in your presence. This

show of respect for the feminine divine energy has now become

the pre-cursor to your day going from tentatively great to

permanently horrid.

One of the uniformed men asks your name in order to confirm to

whom they're speaking; their inquiry is confirmed. They look at each other sullenly, then at you. One of the officers then hesitantly begins his announcement: "Ma'am, your family has been in a car accident. And despite the best efforts of the paramedics, none of them survived." You hear nothing said to you after this. Your mind goes blank. You go blank. And whatever needs to be, or has been, said beyond "none of them survived" becomes immediately moot. You see mouths moving, but their words are now muted. This is what it felt like being diagnosed with Stage I-C Ovarian Cancer.

Monday, January 16th, 2006. A day I remember clearer than my own birthday. A day I remember more than the day I received my bachelor's degree (which took me 6 long ass years to earn). A day that ruined my life in plenty of ways. And as crazy as it sounds, I cannot, nor have I ever been able to comprehend or understand the blessing that was/is supposed to come from something like a cancer diagnosis. I mean seriously: HOW THE FUCK DO YOU REJOICE IN THAT? At 3 weeks shy of turning 23, I had done everything I was supposed to: got a high school diploma; worked a job; partied hard and loved harder; avoided following my mother's example of being a teenaged mother; and treated everyone I knew and loved with respect. I carried myself with integrity, I did not curse in front of children or my elders [often], I volunteered with not-for-profit organizations, and I gave a helping hand when and where needed. You would think these individual acts of kindness would mean something to God. They didn't mean shit. Because all the people who could have been subjected to this type of punishment were missed; the cancer target somehow or another was aimed, purposefully, at me.

So, this is my story. My struggle. My feelings behind my diagnosis, my treatment, and life after that. Hell, the aftermath could double as a whole separate book, but that's another project for another day. On this particular day, we're going to talk about me, my diagnosis of Stage I-C Ovarian Cancer at age 22, how I dealt with it, how I didn't deal with it, how my family and friends were affected, and how I'm doing now almost 13 years later. It's not an easy story to tell. It wasn't an easy thing to experience, and alone for that matter. It's not easy expressing this at all, mostly because it's triggering. I mean, let's get serious here: I've sugar-coated my anger, frustration, and depression behind a mask of smiles and a dissertation worth of wisdom and encouragement. I've done it so much that people around me seem to think that I'm this magical creature. I can do anything for one reason and one reason only: because I beat cancer. And to an extent, they're right.

Here's where things get complex: my sugar-coating leaves room for the masses to negate that I'm human. And I feel things. And shit bothers me. And nouns (people, places, and things) irritate the shit out of me. Somehow or another, beating cancer has made the masses believe that I am now invincible and void of all ability to do anything other than win. In creating the Hero narrative for me, I've inadvertently been stripped of my capacity to be a human being. I can't feel anything other than grateful that I survived. That I was spared by the Universe. That I'm still here to tell my story.

Please tell me how the fuck that has anything to do with my feelings surrounding any of this? My diagnosis has taught me several things; the most pivotal lesson is that people are really fucking selfish. Fuck how you feel; it's all about how they feel, and how they feel you should feel. Fuck the fact that they weren't there with you. Fuck the fact that they have no direct experience. Fuck the fact that, ultimately, I am not them and will not process my experience as they have. I just have to be this beacon of hope. Because they're in desperate need of it. As if I don't need my own damned healing.

This is my truth. This is the real of my experience. This is what happens when the King of All Monkey Wrenches is thrown into your life's plan, with no Plan B to recover with. This is what happened to me, and the aftermath of it.

Y'all get ready for a wild ride.

CROSSROADS

CONTENTS

Chapter I:

<u>Accident Ahead: Expect Delays</u>

It was the end of 2005, and I was riding out the last of my few days on Christmas break. I had noticed a while back that I had gained some weight but thought nothing of it…..that is, until I got home and REALLY took a look at my stomach. I mean, I REALLY, REALLY, REALLY looked at it. Had I been paying any TRUE attention beforehand, I would have seen that I, standing at the bus stop waiting to be dropped off near my best friend's house, could have passed for being, at bare minimum, 4 months pregnant. I stood there, thought, pre-panicked, then calmed down enough to call the best friend that I was going to see and tell her that we may need to take a trip to Walgreens, and I may need to make a phone call to my boyfriend (at the time). My best friend immediately came and picked me up from the bus stop where I was waiting and went on a field trip with me to the nearest pharmacy. I made sure to grab the pregnancy test that had the "two-for-one" tests in it, because I just WASN'T GOING for being pregnant, whether it was already well in the works or past the point of no return. We paid for the test, went back to her house, and I immediately made a beeline for the bathroom. I pissed, I wiped, I cleaned, I washed my hands, I waited....and waited.....and waited......for two whole long ass minutes to receive very relieving, but very confusing, news: both tests immediately came back negative. I sighed for a few reasons, one of them mainly being that I so dreaded the idea of having to make that "Green Mile"-esque phone call, saying "Hey babe, remember that night when we drank that entire fifth of Polar Ice vodka.....weeeeeellllllllll......" I did, however, figure that SOMETHING wasn't QUITE right with me. I mean,

I hadn't used the bathroom in over two days........in all honesty, I had been extremely constipated. To do anything other than lay on my mother's living room couch (which served as my bed/bedroom when I came home from school for whatever random reason I had to come home) was more than painful, so on the couch was where I stayed. My mother, forever the unnecessary nagger, noticed that I had not left the couch at all that week, and decided to say something about it. She sat next to me on the couch and did what she always does while I'm on Christmas break: fuss about my never doing anything more than sleeping and watching TV all day. My mother, with all her beauty, had an ugly contempt for nagging; there were days that she made the worst mothers-in-law look like Mother Teresa. To get up and actually do something during my break (especially when your schedule was as jam-packed as mine had been that year) would be totally against my morals as a college student; I never understood why this was such a point of annoyance for her. So, once she got into full swing with her "This Is the Song That Doesn't End"-esque speech, I tune her out. In a way, her nagging was similar to a popular song to me: after hearing it so many times, it becomes a bit bothersome, forcing you to either eventually tune the song out or turn it off altogether. This time, however, the nagging was for an additional reason: she seemed to attribute my recent stomachaches to my tight-fitting clothing. According to her, the fact that I had damn-near painted my clothes on just HAD to have resulted in my pain. "You aren't exactly a size 9-10 anymore Kawana. You might ACTUALLY be a size 15 now. And those clothes that you call "old women's" clothes MIGHT just be the clothes you have to start wearing from now on. You can't walk around wearing tight clothes ALL THE TIME!!! That is probably why your stomach hurts so much. "I guess I can't blame her for thinking or feeling this way. I did notice that I had picked up some extra weight in the last six months, and I

DID have a tendency to buy clothes that clung to me, but that's always been my preference; I didn't understand why she hadn't caught the clue on that by now, but she was stuck on her theory, so I let her have it. No use in arguing about it. It wasn't gonna take the pain away, and it wasn't gonna shut her up which, by THIS time, I was SURELY PRAYING she would do. I did notice that I had gained a substantial amount of weight within the last six months, but I just figured that I was either pregnant, which was negated by the "negative" test results, or just needed to get my big ass up and do something to drop this weight. Ultimately, I knew that my clothing had ABSOLUTELY NOTHING to do with the pain that I was in but agreed to go along with her to Wal-Mart to get me some "clothes that actually fit" so that the subject could hopefully be dropped. I initially said "no" to the request, but her fussing about the fact that "maybe a little walking around instead of lying on the couch all day will make you feel better" was annoying the full shit out me, so I relented against my better and BODY'S judgment. I hated going shopping with my mother because she had a tendency to take longer than ABSOLUTELY NECESSARY to go where she needed to go and get whatever it was she went to get. I always wondered how the fuck you go somewhere with a list and STILL forget everything that you need. She always "only needed about an hour," which always turned into 2, slid into 3, and dragged into 4, and so forth. In hindsight, I think it was her way of trying to spend time with me, but back then, I saw it as nothing more than another way for her to get on my god damned nerves. I was fine for the first few minutes that I was there, but after twenty minutes or so of trying to walk around with her, the pains in my stomach became more severe, making it that much harder for me to continue walking. Once she saw me leaning over in pain, she let me go sit down; once she saw me DOUBLED OVER in pain after she had completed her shopping, she shut the hell up nagging about how much pain I was or wasn't in or what the cause of the pain was. The pain eventually subsided, and I was okay for the rest of the day and was a little better for a few days after that.

When it was time for me to return to Nashville to finish my last semester of college, my mother was scared to put me on the bus, but after assuring her that I would go to the hospital if the pain got worse, she sent me on my way. Once I got back to Nashville and got settled in on campus, I found that the pain had gotten neither better nor worse, but it was bad enough for me to miss the first three days of class. It was just too painful to get out of bed, let alone walk anywhere past my bathroom door. What did get worse was my body temperature, which kept shooting up to wazoo in the middle of the night. For a while, I thought that I just had the flu because although it was January, I was always burning up. I was tossing and turning all night, and my body felt like it was on fire. This went on for two days; I got so hot on the third night that when I tried to walk a few doors down to ask a neighbor for some water; I never made it past the threshold of my room door. I ended up leaning up against and sliding down the wall next to my room. With my eyes closed, my body steaming, and still sliding down the wall for comfort (it still hurt to stand at this point), I sank into a deep, dark, place that was too hot to comprehend. My brain felt like it was on autopilot, my body felt like it was about to completely shut down from overheating itself. I didn't know what to do or think.....hell, I COULDN'T think because the heat of my body was making me delirious. I didn't have the strength to anything more than sit there and groan from the intense head that radiated from my body. Luckily, that same neighbor and her boyfriend walked past, saw me, and brought me some water to drink and rubbing alcohol to cool my body off. I'd be a liar if I said that either one worked; I was still hot and still halfway delirious. Somehow or another, I was able to fall asleep which, by this time, had turn into a task all in its own. I didn't understand why, but I started to notice that I could no longer lie on my stomach; whatever was making me look pregnant was also solidifying in my abdomen to the point that even lying on my side was shifting, and irritating, the mystery wrapped in my belly.

The following morning, a Thursday to my recollection, I woke up to my boyfriend walking into my room, fully energized, chipper as hell, saying "Well babe, you ready to go to the hospital?" I had told him that if I hadn't felt better by Thursday, I would go to the hospital. Thursday was here, and I didn't feel better. He must have known that ahead of time, because when he walked into my room, I was still asleep in bed, not ready to do anything more than stay asleep in bed. I got up, got dressed, and proceeded to go to a hospital that was conveniently located across the street from my college. We were seen immediately but sat there for close to 5 hours as the doctors, nurses, and nursing students poked, prodded, and annoyed the hell outta me with questions I didn't have an answer to. Imagine how irritated I was as I sat through multiple blood, urine, and pelvic tests with a dozen or so med school students staring down the barrel of my vagina through my open legs on the examination table. What was even more irritating was when the doctors kept asking me if I were pregnant. Now, that, at that particular point, was the dumbest question that I had heard all day, seeing as though every test that was administered came back negative for it. All I could think was "Man, they must be slacking on their pimpin' with their students here if these dumb fucks keep asking me questions that they apparently already have the answers to!!!" At that point, I just knew that either something was wrong with them, or something was seriously wrong with me. The doctor that was examining me interrupted my thoughts by telling me that my stomach was abnormally firm for me NOT to be pregnant, so they wanted me to a pelvic ultrasound just to be sure that nothing else was wrong. I let them perform the ultrasound, which came back positive for ovarian cysts: not the BEST news in the world, but definitely not the WORST either. All that mattered to me by then was the fact that I had heard some relatively tangible "news" period. This let me know that it was now safe to breathe. But because of the outcome of the ultrasound and my firm abdomen, I was admitted into the hospital for further observation, given a room, and left with nothing but the fifteen Papillion thoughts swirling through my head.

As day melted to night, my temperature rose again, topping out at 105 degrees Fahrenheit. This prompted my nurse to run another urine test, which I was neither looking forward to nor happy about. It would have been totally different if all I had to do was go to the bathroom, piss in a cup, and hand the cup to the nurse while she skipped out of my room with it, excited about what new germs she would discover in my urine. As usual, I had to do it the hard way. I was given a catheter, the second one in less than 12 hours, and the second worst pain that I've ever felt in my life. The first time that it was done earlier that day, I asked why I couldn't just piss in a cup like a normal person. It was explained to me that the urine that comes out the "normal" way is filtered by the body's own processes, and the catheter allows the doctors to examine the unfiltered urine for any abnormalities. Of course, I consented, and hoped that I don't almost die THIS time like I almost did the FIRST time it was done. A catheter (for those relatively normal people that aren't medically "aware") is a long, hollow, slender tube with a diameter no wider than a string of spaghetti. The nurse inserts the tube into a woman's cervix, threading it to the woman's bladder, where the unfiltered urine is located. If I ever run into the idiot that invented this instrument of death, I will not hesitate to slap the blue fuck out of them. Things like that, pain like that, should be considered cruel and inhumane torture. I haven't had the joy of the pain of childbirth, but having something like this done is almost like, what I would imagine to be, giving birth in reverse: instead of something trying to shove itself out, you're letting someone shove something in. If I were a donkey, I would have bucked the nurse that was performing the procedure, even while she was being patient with me and trying to keep me calm. She took the contents of my bladder to be tested, but nothing changed: this test came back negative just like all the others. The doctors could not ignore the firmness of my abdomen, however, so they arranged for me to have a CAT scan to see if there was anything inside of me that couldn't be seen by the naked eye or felt by the naked hand. But before I could even have the procedure done, I had to consume this white substance that was supposed to make it easier for the doctors to see what needed to be seen on the CAT scan. It was like having to drink two gigantic cups of Orange-flavored *Milk of Magnesia*, neither of which stayed in my stomach for very long. The doctors told me that I had to drink both bottles of that mess, but after getting through half of one bottle and throwing it back up, I poured the other bottle in the garbage can next to my bed, hoping that no one would notice it.

After consuming enough to please the doctors, they wheeled me to another section of the hospital for the CAT scan. I was super scared when they started to back me into that great big machine, mainly because I'm claustrophobic above and beyond belief. All I could think to do was cry because I just KNEW that this machine was either going to cause me some other type of special pain or swallow me whole. As I lay in the tunnel while the machine scanned my body, I thought to myself, "I hope that they don't find anything TOO serious." …………… wishful thinking is QUITE the bitch, isn't she………………………...?

About an hour or so after the CAT scan was performed, one of the several doctors that were examining me came to my room to break the news: what made the doctors think I was pregnant was actually a tumor, a rather large one at that. They explained to me that they had found a tumor in my abdomen that was the size of a five-month-old fetus. This description would have been all fine and dandy had I actually been pregnant at one point or another in my life, or even knew what size a five-month-old fetus is supposed to look like; I requested that it be explained to me like my IQ isn't above average. I wish I hadn't done that; the dummy term's size was a lot larger than what I would have ever expected it to be. I was told that the tumor was essentially the size of a full-grown pineapple, which was a bit more tangible to me, but a bit scarier as well. Pineapples tend to be rather large in size, so to imagine something of that size having had invaded my body was a bit disturbing to me. They went on to tell me that I would have to have emergency surgery the following morning. To say that I was floored is an understatement. A TUMOR? Where the HELL did this come from? When you receive news like this, the doctors tell you to ask them anything if you have any questions, but to my amazement, I was speechless. I couldn't fix my mouth to breathe, let alone speak. I was just told that there was a foreign object in my body that had to be removed......immediately....... this is not something that one can take with a grain of salt. It's not like they told me that I was just severely bloated then gave me a ginger ale to burp up the excess gas. I didn't know what else to do or think about it, so I called my parents and told them the news. My mother made it a point to be at the bus station two hours after I called and broke the news to her; she was on the bus two hours after that. She was by my hospital bed by 5am the day of my surgery. I wasn't exactly terrified about the surgery but having her there to make laugh was certainly a relief. Seeing and having her there was the happiest I've ever been to see my mother. Not that I didn't like being around her on any other occasion but being around her at that moment made me realize no matter how much she raked my nerves, or how much she may have wanted to choke the shit out of me on occasion, at the end of the day, the bridge that connects us is love.

My FATHER on the other hand.......... well, our conversation didn't go as Happily Ever After as it did when I broke the news to my mother. When I told my father that I had to have surgery and wanted him there, to my recollection, he mentioned something about either not WANTING to come or not NEEDING to come right at that moment because my mother was there. Now, this isn't to speak negatively about my father at all; he's a wonderful man and is that much more wonderful of a father. To say I am a "daddy's girl" would be putting it extremely lightly: I basically worship the ground that my father walks on. But for their own personal reasons, which I will not dispel out of respect for them, my parents seem to..............well, I'll say this: with their both being Christians, they love each other out of their obligation to do so by the words of Jesus Christ. Personally, I could give a shit what problems that they have or had with each other at that time; all I knew was that I needed them both, and to NOT be there was NOT an option for me. So, for my father to use my mother as an excuse as to why he wasn't granting my request sent me reeling. I remember getting off the phone with him and immediately calling my older brother, Dion, and, through venting, letting my father have it. I don't even recall what came flying out of my mouth, but whatever it was prompted my father to call me back about fifteen minutes later. I remember him saying, "So you called Dion talking bad about me, huh?" I laughed and cursed to myself at the same time. On the one hand, all I could do was chuckle; my father had seemed to fold to my tantrum. I thought it was kind of cute. On the other hand, all I could think was "Sooooooooooooo, it took for me to call my brother and talk bad about you for you to decide to come? That's how you feel??????????????" I'll admit it: I was being a brat. It was explained to me later that he had to figure out a way to get to me with work and money and transportation now a main concern of his. He was going to come, just not that day..........

A couple of hours after my mother arrived some nurses came in and helped me onto the bed that would take me to the operating room. Someone pulled out a needle and jammed it into my shoulder and told me that whatever was in the syringe would help me to relax. It relaxed me alright: not long after I received the shot, this extreme feeling of euphoria came over me, so much so that I started singing as they wheeled me into the operating room. My mother and all the nurses seemed to think that this mini-concert was pretty funny because I remember hearing a lot of laughter amidst my drugged-up state. One I got into the operating room I was transferred onto another bed and told by someone to count backwards from 100 while they lowered a gas mask over my face; I never made it past 98. After several hours that felt like five minutes passed, I woke up to someone calling my name, and to a pain that I didn't realize was legal in the United States until I woke up to it at that moment. It felt like I had said Candyman in my sleep five times, and he popped up and did what he's most famous for doing to those that dare call him aloud. The pain shot from my pelvis to my chest, which wasn't far off from where the actual incision was made. The pain surrounded me like a deep, dense fog, and seemed to enjoy my company, because it wasn't willing to leave, no matter how much I cried and fussed about it. Some nurses wheeled me into my room, and the first thing that I noticed was a very familiar fragrance in the air: it was my boyfriend's cologne. Apparently, he had made it to the room before I did and had been waiting there for me to get out of surgery. I called out to him, and before I passed back out, I heard him say in his tenor voice "I'm right here, baby......" When I awoke, my father was by my bedside, along with my mother and brother. Daddy looked like he had seen a ghost......tired, heavy, sick. I was happy to see my "baby brother," as I had not seen him in a while and wasn't expecting him to be there. I believe I passed out not long after seeing and talking to them, and a couple of hours later, the surgeon came into my room. I believe at this point, the only people that were in my room were my mother and me. My brother and father had gotten hungry and went on a fieldtrip for food. The surgeon came in, introduced herself, and told me that she was one of the surgeons in my operation. She explained to my mother and I that the tumor that I had was classified as an immature teratoma, one of the more rare tumors that can develop in a person. She said that the tumor had developed from some very active cells in my body that decided to commence with the multiplying temper-tantrum that it was throwing inside my body. Unfortunately for me, the temper tantrum that my body cells were throwing developed into the rather large tumor that was found in my abdomen. This particular tumor also has the tendency to grow thing: human hair, teeth, and cells to be exact. My tumor had developed all three. What blew me the most was when the doctor told me that brain cells had been found on the tumor. Because I was still somewhat intoxicated from the anesthesia, I could not make logical sense out of how cells from my brain had made their way all the way down to my midsection. It didn't dawn on me that stem cells had transferred the cells from my brain to the tumor until immediately after the doctor said something.

She went on to explain to me that not had they removed the tumor, but they also had to remove my appendix, my left fallopian tube, and my left ovary. This made me more than a little upset because I thought that I wouldn't be able to have children later. The only thing I could think to do was call my boyfriend in tears, whining about how I may not have been able to have kids; I was reassured by the surgeon later on that because I was so young and still have one good ovary left, I should be fine.

It was the next bit of news that I received that bothered me the most, and still bothers me to this day. The operating surgeon informed me that I was late in Stage one of Ovarian Cancer. I wasn't sure how to take this bit of news; it took a while for it to sink in, I don't think that I realized until later on down the line how serious this news was, and how it would affect me. I don't remember thinking that I was going to die. I think that I thought about the fact that the disease that I had is a disease known for killing people, whether slowly or quicker than humanly possible.

One of the two things that got me through the rest of my time in the hospital is the visitors that I had. My school was directly across the street from where I was located, so I had a steady flow of people in and out of my room, all day and every day. The other thing that got me through my stay there was the morphine drip that was connected to my arm. Pain and I were never really good friends, so anything other than slight discomfort annoyed me past the point of tolerance. Once I did start to feel some type of pain from the fresh incision in my stomach, I'd press the button that administered the morphine, sat back, relaxed, and drifted off to a world where none of this was happening to me. I took a liking to the pain pacifier so much that I would wind up pressing the button between three and five times per pain sensation. There were times that I would be talking to someone in my room, and once the pain kicked in, I would stop all conversation, press my magic button, and do everything short of slip into the most wonderful of all comas in mid-conversation. One of my good friends and singing partners came to see me. I heard him call me by his nickname for me, "….NA-NA!!!!!!!" I looked up through drugged and sleep-hazed eyes, smiled, called out his name, and fell back into my "coma." My friends and family did what they could to treat me as if everything were normal, as if they weren't trying to have a conversation with me hooked up to a morphine drip and anti-biotics. I had a friend bring her laptop in and show me the newest episodes of a cartoon sitcom called "The Boondocks." I adore the show, and worship its humor, but ignorance THAT hilarious and staples as FRESH as mine do not make a good combination; instead of laughing my usual full, hearty laugh, I was too occupied trying to stifle my laugh because laughing caused my stomach to stretch and my staples to move. The company was appreciated, however, as it did tend to get lonely in that room with just my mother and I sometimes. I had a constant barrage of professors, friends, and classmates in and out of my room, making me laugh, bringing me snacks and treats, mailing me cards and flowers, and delivering messages of well-wishes. My friends and I tend to get pretty loud when we're laughing and joking, so it's no surprise that they were asked to leave by the nurses on call; to my recollection, my guests were asked to leave my room on more than one occasion. Once I was released from the hospital, I returned to my dorm room and my mother returned home. I was still in a lot of pain because of the staples in my stomach, but I was also suffering from a severe case of insomnia, so once I was released and my mother returned home, I was left alone: with my thoughts, with my pain, with my open eyes that, by biological nature, were begging to be closed. I couldn't sleep to save the life of me, so I sat up, and found a movie to watch. This didn't aide in my attempt to fall asleep, so I decided to get up and unpack. I unpack....and cleaned......and folded.......and organized.......and consolidated. By the time I had finished with my tasks, it was 5 am.

As school progressed and the word spread about what had happened to me, it became clear to me that I was still considered a student, so I had a shit-load of work to catch up on. My mom went to all of my professors and got the work that I missed for that week, having politely cussed out one of my professors because of his inability to understand that I was missing class because I was in the hospital. But I found that trying to do the work or reading anything was very difficult. I couldn't concentrate because of al the pain that I was in, so I ended up just putting the books down and sleeping off the residual pain from the hospital. A couple of weeks passed before I went back to the hospital to have my staples removed. Once they were gone, one of the other operating doctors informed me that I would have to start my chemotherapy sessions within the month. It was at this moment that I had to make a decision as to what I was going to do about my schoolwork, a decision that I really didn't want to have to make. I was beyond determined to finish school; it had taken me five years and three schools for me to get my degree, and I was willing to do what it took to finish out with the rest of my class. So, in my own stubbornness, I tried to catch up on my reading and class work. I found, however, that the more I tried to read and concentrate on the material, the more frustrated I became. It had become that much more difficult to read, or even focus on anything that I was reading or doing at the time. The pain and fatigue crept in, and made its home in my brain, making it virtually impossible for me to do anything but sleep. The few hours that I could stay awake were filled with visitors, laughter, and smiles, most of them coming from those that came to see me. I don't recall ever being in that much of a smiling mood; I was always just kind of there, filling a void of empty space.

In the few hours that I was awake with no visitors, I knew that I had to make a decision about what would become of the remainder of my semester in undergrad. I knew that I only had a few classes to finish and a recital to prepare for, but I also knew deep down that, as much as I tried to convince myself that I could finish in time to walk, it really wasn't an option for me anymore. With me starting chemo in a little under three weeks, there was no way that I would have the time or strength the finish out that semester with my class. I fought with that decision for a few days before the better half of my brain told me that withdrawing from school was the only thing left for me to do. So, with tears in my eyes and pain in my heart, I went to the provost and informed her that I would be withdrawing for the remainder of the semester. I had never cried so hard....my heart had never felt so heavy. I walked into her office with my withdrawal form in my hand, but my brain couldn't comprehend what I was about to do. I went to her office, requested to see her, and once I stood up to explain to her what my situation was, it hit me exactly what I was about to do. I've never had a piece of paper feel like a piece of steel in my hand......that is, until that moment. She looked me in eyes, and after recognizing me, she asked what she could do for me. I went to hand her the withdrawal form and tell her what I was doing there, but I didn't even get halfway through my sentence before I broke down in tears. I managed to not turn it into a whole sob session, handed her the form, told her about my diagnosis, and the chemotherapy that I would have to take thereafter. I had to track down a few professors, but I FINALLY got all the things that I needed to make my withdrawal official. I was given the blessing of being allowed to remain on-campus for the duration of my treatments by a few powers-that-be that I had built a good rapport with while still a student. That was a relief; where I was going to stay was one thing that I neither wanted nor needed to be worried about. What I did need to worry about was the new venture that I would be embarking on in the weeks coming; a venture that was full of the unwanted than it was full of the unknown.

Chapter II:
Closed for Construction

A few days later, my boyfriend accompanied me back to the doctor's office so that I may have my staples removed and receive the news about my chemotherapy sessions and when they were supposed to begin. The first thing that was done once I got to the office was have my staples removed by an intern. This didn't seem like it would be too painful…. that is, until he started having to do a little work to remove a handful of them. My skin had begun to heal, which means that it was scabbing over the staples, making them more difficult to remove. Apparently, when you're in medical school, the professors don't teach you how to ease your way into a painful situation because this young man kept "easing" the damn staples out of my incision as if what he was doing DIDN'T hurt. Before I had a chance to slap him, he finished removing all of the staples, and sent me on my merry way.

I walked into the office not knowing what to expect. At this point, my entire mental state was "Ok, I'm not dying.......? Ok good....... NOW FIX IT!!!!!!!" Not exactly the BEST way to think of things, but it's all that I COULD think. In hindsight, it was the only thing my mind would allow me to think. I doubt very seriously that I would have been able to cope with letting the fact that a deadly disease had crept its way into my body sink into my head. The moment that I heard my surgeon say "chemotherapy," I think my entire being immediately went into defense mode. The doctor that was to become my gynecological oncologist (dummy terms: consulting chemotherapy doctor for reproductive cancers) walked into the office with a serious look, that melted into a smile the moment she extended her hand to shake mine. She introduced herself as Dr. Khabele as she half flowed, half skipped to her desk. Once she sat down, she explained to me the type of chemotherapy that I had to take, the length of time that I would have to take it, and how it would be administered. She explained to me that because I was so young, and the cancer was caught so early, that I would only have to do three months of chemo. All of the cancer was removed when my fallopian tube and ovary were removed, but the chemo was highly suggested so as to rid my body of any remaining cancer cells that may have been floating around.

She told me that I would be taking 3 rounds of chemo, which equated to about three and a half months of intensive chemotherapy. I would have to undergo what is called outpatient chemotherapy once a week for three weeks; the fourth week would be designated to what is called inpatient chemotherapy. The inpatient was different from the outpatient in that I would be admitted to the hospital for 5 days; in those five days, my chemotherapy sessions were administered every single afternoon. I would be released from the hospital on the last day of my inpatient, just to turn around and have to do a round of outpatient less than five days later. Sounds like a lot, huh? Trust me, when I heard what I would have to do, I thought, "Well, damn: are they TRYING to kill me???? They could not just let the cancer fester for all this shit!!!!!!!" Dr. Khabele explained to me that the downfall of my cancer being caught so quickly was the intensive chemotherapy sessions I would have to undergo. When she told me what TYPE of medicine would be given to me, I didn't think too much of it. I figured that all cancer patients, at one point or another, have to have multiple antibiotics running through them at once. She told me the names of the three specific anti-EVERTHING drugs that would be given to me: bleomycin (an anti-tumor antibiotic; in dummy terms: this drug will keep the tumor cells away), etoposide (an anti-DNA-dividing antibiotic; in dummy terms: DNA, somehow or another, sends a signal to one's cells to

47

divide-etoposide prevents this signal from reaching the cells, which, in turn, prevents cell division and, ultimately, another tumor), and cisplatin (see latter explanation, please and thank you). I can't say that I WASN'T nervous; I honestly don't really remember feeling any emotion about any of this news until I thought about my hair: IT WAS GONNA FALL OUT!!!!!!!!!!!!!!!!!!!!!!!!!!!!!!!!!!!! Of course, I asked if the chemo would take my hair out as if I didn't already know that the answer would be yes. I KNEW that's all that I cared about because the thought of losing my hair made the fact that I had cancer that much more real to me. I finally broke down after two whole weeks and cried like a baby in that office. I wasn't necessarily worried about the fact that I would lose my hair; ask anyone that knows me, and they will tell you that I will chop my hair off with the quickness. It was what I was losing my hair to that made it that much more devastating for me. I mean, it wasn't like I was getting a pixie cut or a Chinese bob......I was getting a Mr.-fucking-Clean!!!!!!!!!!!!!!!!!!!!!!!!!!.................over some BULLSHIT!!!!!!!!!!!!!!!!!!!!!!!!!!!!!!!!!! But I managed to suck it up and make myself accept what I was about to go through. I THOUGHT I knew....... but I had NO IDEA.......................

By the time I was released from the hospital about two weeks prior, the entirety of my campus was abuzz with "news" about my diagnosis; apparently, I had everything from a deadly venereal disease to brain cancer. All this did was further what I had already believed about the college after having been there for over three years: people have absolutely nothing to do with their lives but sit around and figure out what was wrong with me instead of coming to and asking me, the only person that really knew the entire story. There were two incidents that I dealt with once I returned to school, the first being a young lady that approached me as I was leaving my dorm. Here I was, going to sit on the yard, toddling down the stairs, minding my own business, when I look up and see a familiar-looking girl that I knew through a few friends. She stopped me and asked me my name as if she didn't already know it. When she asked me, she had this smile on her face as if she was going to hand me a damn paycheck. I HATE when people try and play a role that they really aren't. According to her, she had heard around campus that I had been talking about her, that she didn't understand why I had anything bad to say about her, and if I had a problem with her, I could have easily come to her room to speak to her about it. I swiftly told that silly bitch that had she had a LIFE, she would have known that I was in the hospital being diagnosed with cancer, so there was no way that could have said anything about her. I hadn't even been on-campus to want to say anything about her. I didn't know anything about her past her and her boyfriend's name and made it very clear to her that I honestly didn't give enough of a shit about either of them to know or want to know anything past that. I proceeded to politely tell her to get a fucking life, get the fuck out my face with the bullshit, and excuse my back as I find something important to converse with someone about. This incident was lightweight, however, compared to the betrayal that I felt from a young lady that I considered my close friend at the time. Word on the street was that she was the reason that people on campus believed that I had cervical cancer, which is known to be caused by a sexually transmitted disease or infection. Apparently, while I was in the hospital, she and her mile-a-minute mouth-having ass roommate were sitting around speculating about what I did or didn't have in a room full of people that I really didn't even speak to. By the time she and her roommate had finished running their fucking mouths about me, I just HAD to have gotten "burned" (infected by an STD/I) because I hung around so many guys that I just HAD to be fucking at least two of them, one of which had to have given me whatever it was they thought I had. The amazing thing about one of the young ladies was the fact that she was a biology major......obviously the most stupid one I've ever come across. Had she asked, she would have known that my cancer was of the ovaries, which, by this time, wasn't new news to anyone, not even the faculty. What was even more amazing to me was the fact that the entire time that the "friend" had been talking about me, she was coming to visit, dropping off treats, and leaving me letters letting me know that she had stopped by and that she loved me: basically, she was being phony as fuck, smiling in my face and slamming me past my hairline. But this is what happens when you deal with simple bitches with the label of "friend" that isn't truly understood.....this is what happens when you assume......this is what happens when bitches have nothing to do but sit around and run their fucking mouths about shit instead of either finding some fucking homework to do or coming to the source........whew, sorry, still a little salty about that whole situation. But hell, wouldn't you be? I mean, come on: someone you consider a close friend of yours is slandering your name instead of defending who you are and what you have. To add insult to injury, they're smiling in your face as if they didn't FRESH finish talking bad about you. If that isn't the deepest sense of betrayal, I don't know what is....

I was given about a week to prepare for my chemotherapy sessions.... a week to live a normal life, one that I wouldn't be able to live anymore after I finished my rounds. I don't really recall what I did during that week, but I recall the first day that I started chemotherapy. A very long day, it was. The first day that I had to "report for duty," I was a ball of emotions, none of them necessarily good; they were more anticipatory than anything else. I walked into the waiting area and was asked to fill out the usual booklet of paperwork: name, address, contact information, and next of kin: things like that. As I sat there and filled out the Spanish

Inquisition of paperwork, I couldn't help but think about what I was there for: I was there because I had CANCER!!!!!!!!!!!!!!!!!!!!!!!!!!!!!!!!!! Right now, I'm supposed to be complaining about having to study for finals. Right now, I should be dragging my ass to the music building to practice for my upcoming Senior Vocal Recital. Right now, I should be helping my sorority sister prepare for our Greek Week. Right now, I should be trying to pack for an out-of-town trip with the Jubilee Singers. Right now, I should be smiling about how close my walk across the stage to FINALLY receive my degree after 5 years was. But where the fuck WAS I instead.........at the hospital, trying to figure out when, in my life, did God decide to say, 'FUCK YOU' to me. I sat, filling out the paper, and the more I looked at it all, the more I thought about what I had, the more I thought about what I was about to undergo, the more freely the tears fell from my eyes. Once I finally finished all the paperwork and handed it in, I was asked to relocate to the section of the hospital where my blood was to be drawn. This shouldn't have irritated me as much as it did; with the nurses having to take my blood at least 3 times a day before I was diagnosed, I should have been used to it. But when the veins in your arm are all but nonexistent because of the constant and consistent blood work being done, you don't look forward to the impending prick of the needle. My left arm had had so much blood work done on it that one would think that I was a heroin addict with a deathly bad habit. Blood was taken from that particular arm so much that after a few months or jabbing and sticking, that the veins eventually just flattened out and died. I can't recall the last time that blood was taken from my left arm. So, to say that I was pissed when the nurse reached for my left arm to do the blood work is lightweight. She jabbed, she maneuvered, pulled out, jabbed again, maneuvered, found a vein, got my blood, bandaged me up, and then sent me to another section of the hospital where my PICC line would be put in. When a person has to undergo chemotherapy, they have three manners in which it is administered: antibiotics through a port-a-catheter (which is located in an opening in one's chest area), radiation (when the medicine is administered in a matter that tends to burn your skin), and antibiotics through a PICC line (which is what was given to me). A PICC line is basically a long piece of tubing that is threaded through your arm to an aorta in your heart, where the antibiotics would go and disperse themselves throughout your bloodstream, killing the cancer cells in your body. I was taken to a room with some big, scary-looking machine, and told to undress from the waist up......fine with me; I hate clothes anyway. After swiftly snatching my shirt over my head with my bra to follow soon after, I sat and waited for the doctor and his nurse to return to the room, and once they did, I was told to lie down on the big, scary-looking machine. As soon as I got comfortable on the table, I was told to place my arm in this stirrup-looking thing that didn't allow me to see past my shoulder. Once this was done, I was given a local anesthetic......VERY local. Not long after the anesthetic was administered, I felt this thin, sharp, pain shoot through my upper arm. It almost made me sit up and start cursing, but the pain got thinner and deeper, so the only thing I COULD do was shed a tear, sit back, and pray that this whole ordeal would be over soon. When the doctor was finished, my PICC line was firmly in place. I was finally allowed to sit up and look at my arm, from which the receiving end of the PICC line was dangling, being held to my arm by a piece of gauze tape. After this was done, I was escorted to the section of the hospital that was to become my second home for the next three months.

I walked into the chemo administration room, and was greeted by friendly faces, full of smiles, concern, and warmth. I don't quite remember what the main nurse's name was, but I remember that she was always particularly nice to me. She was always patient in explaining to me all the medicines that I would have to take, the side effects that I would be affected by, how long each session would take. She brought me to the room where the patients would receive their dosage of death and showed me to a chair. The room was filled with about 8 or 10 recliner chairs, equipped with an armrest. All of the chairs faced towards the back of the room on a diagonal angle so that all the patients could partake in whatever episode of "Jerry Springer" was on at the time. There was another section just like this on the outside of the room, except the chairs and beds were located in an open area instead of an enclosed room. I was taken to the enclosed room, sat down, and given a cap of three pills: an Advil (as a prophylactic), Benadryl (as a sedative), and some random other pill. I took the pills, sat back, and tried to relax as the nurses set up my dosage for the week. Luckily, this was an outpatient session, so although I was there for over 6 hours, the sessions themselves would only last about 3 hours. Once

I was all hooked up to my meds, the session began. I watched as the antibiotics and other various medicines slowly, but surely, disappeared from the bags where they were located into my arm. I was fine for the first hour or so, but as the drugs started to intermix with my blood, I started to feel some type of woozy way. I don't remember much about that day......I passed out about an hour into the session. When I awoke, it was 4 in the afternoon. I went to jump up because I had remembered that one of my girls was waiting downstairs to drive me back to my dorm room. Once I realized that she had probably already come and gone (and that I was still connected to the machines), I relaxed for all of five more minutes before I got up, called her back, and asked her to meet me back at the hospital. Of course, I got lightly cursed out, but she understood why I didn't come downstairs while she was waiting on me. She wasn't sure where in the hospital I was, and the signal of my phone was pretty weak in the room where I was, so all she could think to do was go back to campus frustrated. After that, we created a system: I figured that my chemo sessions would last until about 12:30, so she would just come and pick me up after I was done. The ride was always appreciated because the drugs, particularly the Benadryl, made me very woozy and disoriented. I remember calling my boyfriend after one particular outpatient session, and I was slurring so badly that I had to repeat what I had said to him about three times. I didn't think it would be that hard to say "Hey babe, I just got out of my chemo sessions. The medicine has me really tired, so I'm gonna go and lie down." I guess it sounded more like Mushmouth talk to him. It got to a point where I didn't want to HAVE to depend on my friends, or ANYBODY for that matter, to get me to and from my sessions. I stopped taking the Benadryl (and after a while, all the pills that were being given to me altogether) so that I would be sober enough to be able to walk back to campus on my own. Sitting and thinking about it now, I guess you can say that it was me just trying to find some sense of independence. I already knew that I would have to depend on too many others for too many other things; I wanted to feel like I could do some things on my own, even if I weren't necessarily supposed to.

The one thing that DID annoy me about the PICC line itself was.... the PICC line itself. It was ALWAYS IN THE FUCKING WAY!!!! When I turned my head, when I rolled over in bed, when I ate, when I put my clothes on, when I took my clothes off, when I took a breath.........it was just always THERE. I had to start thinking of creative ways of taking care of my personal hygiene. Not that I COULDN'T wash myself up, or that I walked around smelling like a dump site; I always made it a point to stay as clean as possible because of the drugs resonating from my pores and to keep from getting sick. But I couldn't take a shower because it would get both the PICC line and the bandage that covered it wet. That meant possible infection, and possible reinsertion of a new line. Neither option sounded appealing to me. So, I had to start washing up over the sink of my dorm bathroom. I'd take a dry-off towel and lay it across the floor. Then, I'd turn on the hot water and lather up a wash cloth and clean up. But even this got annoying; I missed the heat and steam and massage of a shower, versus the halfway freezing but warm in portions quick-scrub. Some days, I'd take one of my big dinner bowls, warm the water in a microwave located across the hall from my room, and give myself a GOOD scrub-down. The PICC line didn't seem so very intrusive on days like this; I felt normal on days like this. But I still longed for the days that I could wash myself without having to work my way around an extra appendage. One day, in the middle of the night while I was hanging out with some friends in my room, I casually mentioned missing being able to take a bath....one friend immediately told me to pack a bag and to come back home with her; I could take a bath there. I ran out the door behind her....... any chance I had to feel normal beyond the obviousness of my disease, I grabbed.

The outpatient sessions weren't particularly bad; I usually got in and out of them in a timely fashion. What was bad was the fact that after my first outpatient session, my white blood cell count took a serious nosedive. Apparently, the medicine in chemotherapy not only kills bad cells, they tend to deplete the good cells as well. I was informed that for each time that the cells dropped as dramatically as they did, I would have to get a shot which was to help boost my white blood cell count. I didn't think much of it; at this point, I still had the "………FIX IT!!!!" attitude. Too bad I didn't think to ask what the side effects were. I'm usually pretty vocal about something when I don't know what it or its purpose it, but by this time, I was guaranteed about 4 or so types of different medicines or antibiotic per session ANYWAY, so one more wasn't a big deal. The nurse pulled out this rocket-looking dispenser with a needle attached to it and jabbed it in my arm. You would think that I would be immune to the constant jabs and stabs of needles by now, but, even with 11 tattoos, I was never really fond of the idea of needles; needles equal pain to me and my threshold for it is paper thin. Naturally, I wanted to slap the shit outta her too, but she was so nice and sweet. I sat back and let the medicines take effect, finished my session, got up, and went back to my dorm as usual. Later on, that night, I started to notice that my body had started to ache. I ignored it, assuming that it was just part of the process of chemotherapy: day after day of meaningless pain and aches coupled with more pain and aches. At the third and final outpatient session for this particular month, I had my blood drawn as usual, and as usual my white blood cells had taken a nosedive. The "sweet" nurse jabbed me again, and I sat back and took it.... again; and again, my body started to ache that very same night. Only this time, the aching became a very severe throbbing. I found out that because white blood cells regenerate in the bone marrow, the friction that the regeneration creates causes enough energy to cause one's bones to ache. Because I had to take them at least every other outpatient session, the pain became increasingly worse; it got so bad on some nights that my entire body would spasm from the throbbing pain. Imagine having a migraine in your bones......then multiply it by 5 per migraine. I didn't realize that one's body could thrust and throw itself so viciously....... the pain always lasted clear through the night, which added to my insomnia, which by this time, was at it's absolute worst since I had been released from my initial surgery.

The inpatient chemotherapy sessions were relatively worse than the outpatient, in that I was required to stay in the hospital for five days versus three and a half hours and receive my treatments on a daily basis. By the time I had started my inpatient chemo, I was assured that God had hated my fucking guts: as usual, I had to do things the hard way. Although the PICC line seemed to be the easiest way to access my blood, the doctors and nurses insisted that my blood just HAD to be drawn from my veins. There was no easy, painless way to draw blood, so every prick hurt. Because the veins in my left arm had all fallen flat, the nurses had to find veins in other, more creative places, one of them being in the upper inset of my right arm. My hand, wrist, upper and lower arm were all victims to the plentiful, and sometimes multiple, needle pricks. Having to do chemo on a daily basis wreaked havoc on my appetite; the chemo had somehow altered my sense of smell to the point where I couldn't eat the hospital food because the mere smell of it literally made me throw up. My best friend had to start bringing me food from outside of the hospital in order for me to eat. The times that she couldn't come, I was given Ensure. The hospital had noticed that I hadn't really eaten any food since I had been admitted. I guess this was there way of trying to make me eat; once I started to throw up the Ensure as well, they left me the hell alone. The chemo made it so that I couldn't digest anything that had citric acid. This meant none of some of my most favorite foods: no pineapples, oranges (or juice of EITHER KIND), tomatoes, or pickles. It was uncommon for me to throw up my food in mid-conversation from having unknowingly ingesting something with citric acid. Nothing major really happened to me while I was doing inpatient, but once I was discharged from the hospital on the fifth day, I had the entire weekend of nausea, soreness, and insomnia to look forward to.........just to have to return to the hospital four days later to do outpatient. To say that I was sick every single day would be putting it lightly. There wasn't a day that I didn't throw up. There wasn't a day that I didn't sleep for over 16 hours a day (on the days that I could sleep). There wasn't a day that I truly had energy to do more than lie in the bed. There wasn't a day that the pain didn't have me in constant tears.

Chapter III:

"Merge to the Right"

I remember the day that I discovered what the chemotherapy had started to do to my hair. By the time I had found out that I was to start chemo, I had already cut out my locks and had the campus barber line my hair into a nicely-shaped fade. I loved my hair as short as it was because it was a way to rub my "better-looking lining" in the face of my male counterparts. I recall walking around a few times and playfully pulling my hair only to pull my fingers back and see little speckles of hair between them. One day, as my boyfriend and I were play wrestling on my bed, I turned my head to get away from a kiss that he was trying to give me, only to be greeted by the flakes of hair that had made their way from the back of my head onto the comforter that covered my pillow. Since the comforter was pure cloth and cotton, you can assume safely that a good amount of my hair was on that comforter. I looked at my hair, looked at my boyfriend (who, by this time, had seen the hair flakes as well), and my mind went blank. As my mind tried to recover from what I had just seen, my boyfriend sighed, looked down, looked back at me with this strange sense of affection, and said "Well, babe, it's starting." Two whole weeks went by before I went anywhere near my hair again. Within those two weeks, my head had started to feel like spiders had gotten hold of my hair follicles with their fangs. My scalp was itching something terrible, honey. I didn't wash my hair, though, because my spirit kept telling me that washing my hair would take the remainder of my hair out. This scared me so that I avoided washing my hair....... for all of two more days!!! That shit was getting WRECKLESS!!!!!! So, while at my best friend's house, I finally made up the courage in my own little brain to try and wash my hair. I got the shampoo, turned on the water, and went to work. It felt like the most wonderful orgasm that I had ever had up to that point and had hoped to have again before I died. I was so into this "orgasm," that I didn't notice how my hair was steadily falling from my scalp with each scratch, each rinse, and each spray of the water. I raised my head from the sink and threw a towel over it. Don't ask me why the hell I did this: I had a fade, so there wasn't really much to dry. My thoughts manifested into what I saw in the mirror: what stared back at me was a monster, NOT me. What I saw staring back at me had my Guggenheim nose, my low, slanted eyes, my medium-high cheekbones, my pink lips, my crooked teeth, my brownish, clay-red skin.......... with a head-full of patches of missing hair, with patches of fuzz here and there, with a head full of hair in the back. I was, essentially, and completely bald from my earlobes forward. I gasped, called my best friend, and caught my breath. When she and our mutual best friend came running down the stairs, I showed them the results of my hair washing.........and fell to my knees in a waterfall of tears. They tried their best to comfort me, "Oh 'Wana, you're still pretty. It's ok....... you're the best-looking bald girl I've EVER seen." This didn't help me any......I was still in shock. I was still crying. I was still hysterical. I still had cancer............. the shit became real for me right then

. After I temporarily got myself together enough to breathe, I grabbed my phone and called my stepfather, begging him to send me some money so that I could buy a wig. There was NO WAY that I was gonna walk around with my head looking like "WHAT THE FUCK..............you LIKE lookin' like that???????????" My stepfather reassured me that my bald head doesn't make me, but that he would send the money immediately. In the meantime, I had my friends take me back to campus, where I tried to gather myself and my thoughts. Once I calmed down enough to coherently speak, I made two phone calls: one to my boyfriend, and the other to my friend, Anjolique. I called

my boyfriend first and let him know what happened. I

called Anjolique and did the same. They both agreed to

stop by and see me the next day. My boyfriend came by

early the next afternoon, but as he entered my already

open door, he didn't think that I was there. That's

probably because I had hidden myself under a pillow and

my comforter; I was ashamed, too ashamed to let him see

me this way. I was frozen in a permanent fetus position

by the time he realized exactly where I was. He removed

the comforter, and I held onto my pillow even tighter. I

didn't want to............. I COULDN'T let him see me

this way, looking like Gollum on a WORSE hair day. I

felt a gentle tug at my arm, and I hugged my pillow even

tighter. I felt the tug again, and I let the pillow go. I

finally sat up, but I had my back to him. He tugged again,

and I finally turned all the way around to let him see the

damage that was done. He looked at me, smiled, and

grabbed me into a hug. He said, "Well, I KNOW you're

hungry......let's go eat. Hey, why don't you throw on

one of those "doobies" that you love so much (a "doobie"

is a piece of fabric or a shirt that's tied around your head

and knotted at the nape of your head)? You look cute in

those. That way, nobody will notice your hair." It was

always like him to keep cool and act like things were ok;

I appreciated that. Hell, I NEEDED it. We went to eat

lunch before he had to return to work, and once he

dropped me off, I ran into Anjolique. She took one look

at my head, and made one phone call to our unofficial

official campus barber, Frank. "Aye yo, Frank, dis

Anjolique, how you?.......... Dat's good........ I'm well,

thank you for asking. Aye listen, Kawana needs a favor.

You KNOW she started chemo, right? Well, her hair is

falling out, and she needs the smoov shave, ya dig? Cuz

she's over here crying, and panicking, and I ain't gon' be

able ta' do it.........ok....... a'ight den. We are coming

over death right now.......

alRIIIIIIIIIIIIIIIIIIIIIIIIIIIIIIIIIIIIIIIIIIIIIIIIIIIIIIGHT, thank you." With a swing of her hair, she said "Let's go......he is waiting on you right now. He said you can go after homeboy that's in his chair now. We 'bout to get 'chu RIGHT boo!!!!!!!!!"

We swiftly walked around a few corners and down a few hallways to arrive at Frank's "shop." His space was at the end of the hallway of the dorm that we lived in, which was a big open space that stretched back from the rooms about 10 feet or so. It had a window that faced at least three different buildings and parking lots located on our campus. It was here that he set up shop, having his instruments either on him in his effectively professional barber's cape or in his effectively professional barber bag, which was always located on the floor to the right of his barber "chair." Located near the bag was his mini-stereo, always pumping some hip-hop (underground or otherwise), neo-soul, or putting us up on other new artists. This was always the part that I enjoyed when I visited Frank. He had given me the fade that I was rocking before my shampooing fiasco, so I trusted his handy work. Plus, I had witnessed and seen his handy work on other students there and a few of my close personal friends, so if I had to have ANYONE shave me down, it would have been him. He and I exchanged the usual formalities; he sat me down, threw the cape over my neck, and went to work. He shaved the remainder of my hair off, and then evened out the bald parts of my hair. When he finished, he asked me if I were ready to see my new 'do. I told him to give me a few seconds......I had to get my life together. I had to ready my brain for what my eyes were about to bear witness to. I took three deep breaths, and said "Ok, show it to me...." He lifted the mirror to my face, and to my amazement, I didn't faint. I looked like I had been digitally altered. It was me, but not me, yet still me. I didn't get mad or sad about it......I kinda smiled, hugged Frank, thanked him, and went back to my room with Anjolique. I couldn't be extremely upset....... I'd rather be bald than Patch Adams around the hairline ANYDAY.

Within three days, I had a check for forty dollars, and was at the nearest costume shop looking at what I figured would be the cutest wig to fit my face. I found one, but even in finding it, trying it on, and wearing it for a couple of days, I started to feel like......well, PHONY. Anyone that knew me that I had grown out of wearing straight hair at the age of 19, so to stand here, now, at 22 with a bone straight wig I started to feel like I was putting up the biggest front on the planet. That wig rubbed my spirit in the wrong way every time I put it on my head; I'd look in the mirror and see....... everything but me. The wig wasn't just causing my spirit discomfort....it was also interfering with the temperature of my body, which, at this point, had started into full swing hot flashes caused by the removal of my left fallopian tube and ovary. I could be at the mall with that damn wig on, and once the hot flashes kicked in, that wig became the main source of heat on my body. I went to a step show with that wig on and swore on the Bible and Koran that everyone was staring at me because they knew I didn't have no damn hair, and the hair that I had definitely wasn't mine. The last time that that wig saw my scalp was when I was at Chili's with two of my really good friends. We were just sitting there, chilling, eating, and catching up, when all of a sudden, I felt this tremendous flash of heat envelop my body. Keep in mind that I was sitting directly under an air duct that was pumping out cold air because of the steadily rising heat outside. All of this meant absolutely nothing; that vent was blowing cold air directly on the back of my neck, and those flashes were STILL slapping me in the face. Every five minutes or so, I would stop in mid conversation and say, "Y'all, I'm REALLY, REALLY hot......." After suffering through this for about thirty minutes, my hand moved to my head before my mind had real time to comprehend what I was about to do. In one fluid motion, I reached up, politely snatched that damn wig off my head, placed it on the corner of the chair located next to me, looked my friend's dead in the eye, and said, "Aye y'all, don't let me forget that." Both they and the table for 10 located a few tables behind us sat there frozen for about 10 seconds. At 11 seconds and some change, one of my friends burst into laughter; the other friend was still in shock. I looked at them both and said, "What, shit, I'M HOT!!!!!!!!!!!!!!!!!!" They continued to laugh, we continued to eat and talk, and we went back to campus, wig in tow, to talk and laugh about it all again. I don't really know what motivated me to snatch that wig off past the fact that it was just too damn hot under all that hair. I think I was just trying to shed myself of the one thing that was making me uncomfortable about having cancer. In my twisted little mind, I felt like wearing a wig was being phony, and phony was something I was not, not even on accident. I didn't necessarily like the fact that I had to walk around bald for God knows how long, but I surely didn't like the idea of being unnecessarily comfortable either. Being bald usually comes with having cancer; that was what it was, and I knew that there was nothing that I could do about it. What I COULD do was to try and be as comfortable as possible, and I was everything but with all that hair on my scalp.

So, from that point forward, I walked around with a bald head. It wasn't the best feeling in the world, but it wasn't the worst either. I don't remember seeing too many people staring DIRECLY at me when I was bald, but I do remember a friend or two always ready to fight because they had caught someone gawking and staring at me. There was a situation where I thought I had lost my I.D. and my mother took me to the DMV to get another one. I got in line, paid for the I.D., sat down, and waited for my number to be called. Once it was called, I took the picture, hairless scalp and all, and walked back towards my mother, who by this time was looking a little flustered. When I asked her what was wrong, she told me about this guy that was sitting behind me before I went to take my photo. Apparently, while he was on the phone, he made mention of me to whomever he was speaking to on the other end. He wondered why I chose to walk around with a bald head. "I mean, she's a pretty girl, and I respect her for even WANTING to do that, but I could never be with a woman with no hair.... I'm just saying......" A woman sitting next to him turned and said, "You dumb ass; if you look at how her hair is growing, you'd see that she's bald because she just finished chemotherapy. She has cancer you fucking idiot!!!!" The man's reply: "I wasn't even talking to you lady.... why are you all up in my business?" That was the worst incident that I had ever run into. Everyone else just asked me why I was bald and what "that" was hanging from my right arm ("that" being the PICC line, which I had so handily hidden with a piece of fabric wrapped around my arm). Once they found out, they'd smile, give me the biggest hug in the world, and ask me a million more questions, then go about their merry way. The funniest thing about being bald was the extra attention that I got from men. I don't know what it was about a bald woman that makes a man flock to them, but I got more compliments from men when I was hairless than I had gotten when I had hair down my back. I went to a local restaurant near my campus and walked in before I realized that I had left my wig in my dorm. I reached for my head, thought to myself, "Oh SHIT, I'm bald in public....... oh well, I'm already in here, and mu'fuckas already see me....and I'm hungry as hell. Fuck them." As I got in line, I saw a police officer staring dead in my face. I looked, raised my eyebrow, turned my nose up, and looked back at the menu. As I finally got to the front of the line, the police officer left. I grabbed my food and walked towards Anjolique's car, but I noticed that the same cop that was staring at me in the restaurant was sitting in front of my car waiting for me. Once he saw me walking towards the car, he got out of his squad and approached me. Of course, I turned him down, but it was funny as hell. On another occasion, I went with some friends to a picnic that was being thrown by a particular fraternity that tends to wear their hair shaved on a pretty consistent basis. So, when I walked up to the picnic and people started to notice me, the fraternity members all flocked towards me. Some of them stared in amazement, others just wanted to come and give me a hug because they thought I looked sexy with a bald head. One man walked up to me, and asked if he could lick my head……. CLEARLY, I laughed in his face. Once they all figured out why I was rocking a bald head, you would have thought that I had grabbed a microphone and said, "Me and Superhead are best buddies, and she taught me everything she knows……wanna see?" These men were flocking to me like flies to fresh dog shit. It was all flattering and overwhelming at the same time. I'm all for relative attention, and even in that case, I'd rather it be at a bare minimum. But it seemed that the one thing that I initially despised the most about this whole process was the one thing that was garnering me the most attention. Maybe I would have been better off wearing the wig after all……. but where would the fun have been in that?

The double-edged sword for me was the support system that I had. Well, it wasn't really the support system itself….it was how extremely protective my friends were sometimes. I mean, they were some monsters, and for good reason. I can understand why they would want to be protective. People are insensitive, and everybody isn't going to understand why the big, clay red-skinned girl was stark bald with a crack pipe hanging from her arm. But there were moments that I just wanted to say, "Well, damn………ain't I still grown? Cancer didn't turn me into a fucking kid……stop following up behind me!!!!!!" There was an incident when I was doing inpatient chemotherapy, and my friend, Rae, stopped by. She came by frequently to check on me, bring me snacks, and watch television with me until I fell asleep throughout the entire process. But she asked as many questions as the day is long in the summertime. You would have thought that she was the one receiving the chemo. I was getting ready to start my treatments, and the nurses had to test my blood first. The nurse that was trying find a vein had a difficult time finding one. She got to her second poke, and Rae jumped right on it. "Uh uh......what's the problem? Why can't you get a vein for her......? hold on a second, you need to go and call another nurse in here.... nurses are only supposed to try for a vein three times, and you are up to number three, and she don't need to be poked all those times. That's unnecessary.... are you sure you know what you're doing? Can you go ahead and call that other nurse in here please?" Another nurse came in, and got a hit in one try, which was a relief to me. I didn't wanna hit her with the anger that I had for the other nurse that kept poking me. But I almost wanted to hit Rae for asking all of those questions; I'm sure there were more, but I blocked them out after a while. I guess I was embarrassed that she was just talking down to the poor nurse, and even more embarrassed that she asked the barrage of questions as boldly and brashly as she did. I felt more like her daughter than her friend. I understand her concern, but I was used to the pokes and prods, so I didn't object. Not that I really could object. I just wished that she didn't give the woman the 22nd degree. Hell, she made ME uncomfortable with all of her questions.

Another incident was when another good friend of mine, Tee, got upset with me one day when she saw me outside on a chilly day with flip flops, no jacket, and no hat on. She went ballistic. She fussed on and on and on about how I should have covered up more, that I was putting myself at risk for being sick. I understand her concern as well, because she was absolutely right. But I was gonna be in a car, so I didn't think I needed a jacket that I was gonna take off after a hot flash hit me anyway. That's why I wore the bald head and sandals too. The chill didn't bother me; I welcomed it, if anything. But this girl got so upset with me that she didn't talk to me for about three days. She even called my mother and fussed about it. I damn-near died of laughter when my mom called me trying to tell me about how Tee was just concerned about me and she cared about my health.

I remember walking around on campus one week and noticing these flyers about a poetry set in our main "auditorium." I immediately got sad because I so craved hearing a good poem, but even with the event costing a dollar, I didn't have the money to attend. Plus, I think that I had something to do on that day at the same time, anyway. On the day of the poetry set, my sorority sister, Ne-Ne, called me and asked me if I wanted to go out to dinner with some sorority sisters of ours. Of course, I said hell yeah; I'm a sorority girl to the marrow, so whatever chance I had to hang out with my sisters, I took it. She told me what time to be dressed and what time she would drop by to pick me up. Later on that evening, she came by like she said she would, but said that she needed to stop by the poetry set because she had to recite a piece that she had written. By this time, I was rolling my eyes; I was too hungry to want to make any unnecessary stops before we ate. But I went along with her. Once we got to the "auditorium," I noticed that two more of my elder sorority sisters were at the set as well. This truly confused me, as they had both graduated almost two years earlier, and were not known for coming on campus for events. Of course, I greeted them anyway, and even took a picture with them. By this time, Ne-Ne had entered the auditorium. About three minutes passed, and I saw my buddy, Brandon walk onto the stage with the microphone. He and I were Jubilee Singers together, and I knew that he was a connoisseur of poetry; I wasn't at all surprised to see him hosting this particular event. What I was surprised at was when he acknowledged me. I heard his baritone voice say, "I see my sister Kawana standing back there…. whaddup girl?" I looked up, raised my eyebrows, wave, say hi, and kept talking to my sisters. Then I heard him say, "Come on in heah, guuuuhl!!!!!!!!" I looked up, half embarrassed because everyone was staring at me; half ashamed because I really didn't have the dollar to get in. I shook my head, said, "Nah, I'm straight." He said, "Come, on Koala Bear (his nickname for me) ……" then, my sisters started pushing me from behind. Once I walked in the door, everyone in the room stood up and started to clap. It was then that I realized that the poetry set was for ME………. I was speechless the entire night. The two sisters that I saw in the hallway walked me down to the front row, center seat. I figured out that they were in on this whole thing too. The "thing" being the poetry set itself; it was actually being planned as a benefit concert for me, but they cleverly disguised it as a "poetry set" so that I may not catch on to what was going on. All of my classmates were there, in support of me. My line sister had to do a piece alright……a piece about ME; she was in on it too. One of sisters from the

Jubilee Singers got up and said a speech that made me cry. Two of the fraternities on campus did a performance for me, one of which I happily participated in. A group of my classmates did a ridiculously hilarious skit for me; I'm glad that they knew that I could appreciate a good laugh….and what a laugh I had. One of my elder sorority sisters came in, and it was like when Bruce Leroy found his inner "glow" in "The Last Dragon." She floated into the auditorium with her golden "glow" and all I could do was smile, cry, and hug her. The Jubilee Singers came, in full performance "uniform," and sang one of my favorite negro spirituals, "An' I Cry……." with me singing the solo, as I usually did when I was traveling with them. To this day, anytime I hear that song, it makes me cry. And I don't mean cry as in get all sentimental…. I mean cry as in somebody died cry. It's always the same reaction…. they're always the same amount of tears. At the end of all the laughs, words, and tears, I was given an envelope: it contained almost $500. My classmates had gotten together and raised some money for me to get by on for the rest of the semester....... I was MORE than grateful. I didn't have MANY moments like this during my bout with chemotherapy; most of the days were filled with pain, a relative amount of sleep, and more pain. But days like this......THINGS like this made the suffering all worthwhile.

As the days passed and the chemo sessions went on, I noticed that graduation day was coming up.... fast. It was a bittersweet memory for me. My class would get to walk across the stage to receive the degrees that they all had worked, sweated, bled, and cried for. Of course, I would be doing the same work, sweating, bleeding, and crying......in my very last chemotherapy session, which was scheduled for the day after graduation. The night before graduation, I was sitting in my room with my boyfriend and the subject of graduation and my last session came up. All of a sudden, in the middle of the conversation, I just burst into tears. I just fell into his chest and wept. I guess all the pent-up emotions that came with having to go through what I had to go through had finally caught up with me. All I could say was, "It was all a waste......all that work I did......it was just a waste......they get to walk, but not me....... I HATE THIS.... I HATE THIS......I HATE THIS!!!!!!!" I don't think I had really cried or felt any type of way about the whole process before that moment. Before that moment, I was in survival mode. I was just trying to get through it all. I didn't think for one second that it would all fall on me as hard and heavily as it did. I had a myriad of reasons for being frustrated, and they all came out in my tears. I cried myself to sleep in his arms that night; I woke up the next morning at the exact moment that graduation ended. I think that was God's way of shielding me from the pain of waking up earlier, only to watch my friends take the obligatory and traditional "yard march" to the graduation site from my dorm. I'm glad that he knew that would have been too much pain for my already shredded spirit to bear. I got out of bed, shook off the cloud of sadness that had gripped my heart, freshened up, and when to go greet and congratulate my classmates. Their festive moods kept me in a festive mood, but deep inside, I was still bitter, and angry, and frustrated. I was happy for them, but jealous of them because they had was I was supposed to have. I didn't let my anger overshadow their days though. I put on my smile, hugged everyone, made my rounds, and went back to my room to prepare for my last session.

The following day was my own PERSONAL day of graduation, however. On May 9, 2006 I received my very last round of chemotherapy. That was the happiest moment of my life. I would have ripped that damn PICC line out of my arm if I knew how to do it. Once I received my antibiotics, I sat anxiously and waited for the nurses to remove the "chain" that made me a temporary slave to this disease. I sat their alert, excited to finally be rid of it all: the disease, the PICC line, the constant sickness, sadness, sleeplessness, sleep fullness, poking, prodding, measuring, taking, taking, and taking. The nurse stepped into my right side, put her hand on the PICC line, and said "Are you ready?" I said "Hell yeah.... I was ready to have it OUT when you put it IN!!!!" By this time, I didn't care that I was gonna be sick for the rest of the weekend, if not for at least another week. I didn't care that I wouldn't start back growing hair until August of 2006 (head, eyebrows, eyelashes, leg, arm, galore). All I cared about was being rid of that nuisance. She removed the bandage that covered the line and slowly pulled it out of the incision in my arm, which by now had formed into more of a narrow, tubular hole. The first and only thing that I could think after "I'M FREE!!!!!!!!!!!!!" was "Whew.......my arm smells like an open bag of dirty ass cracks......I will DEFINITELY be taking a shower tonight........."

EPILOGUE

You would think that after finishing chemotherapy that my life would return to normal. It didn't. It couldn't have. Because by the time I had completed chemo, what I considered "normal" was no more. I was nowhere near the same person I was post-chemo that I was pre-chemo. And it showed. Yeah, I went back to school and finished, but I was fucking miserable the entire time. Mostly because…. well, my ass shouldn't have returned back to school so soon for starters. I needed that time to recover from, what I now know was, a traumatic event. I realize that now. But back then, my only concern was returning to school. It was all that mattered. It should have been the last thing on my mind; it wasn't. I did go on to graduate in May of 2007, but I was not the same Kawana walking out that I was walking in. There was no more optimism. There was no more cheerfulness. There was no more sense of humor. There was no more warmth. There was no remanence of Kawana left; the slivers of me that were left were so stretched and so damaged that nothing would have repaired them. Then things got worse; real life kicked in. And fast.

I had nowhere to stay immediately after graduation. And where I was staying, I was asked to leave for overstaying my welcome. When I did finally find housing and employment, my anxiety and depression set in so severely I'm surprised that I was able to function. Things got so bad for me emotionally that at one point I put a knife to my wrist and attempted suicide. I was so over life and angry about my diagnosis by that point that death was preferred and welcomed with open arms. I was tired of being angry. I was tired of crying every day, all day. I was tired of my memory failing me (because "chemo fog" is real). I was distraught over the dissolution of my 3-year relationship due to infidelity on his part. I was so over life that I intended to kill myself in hopes that someone would check on me and find my body. I was that done with life, and how fucked up it became because of something like a cancer diagnosis. Nobody could relate to me, so who could I talk to? Nobody in my circle had ever experienced this, so why talk to them about it? They had their own shit to deal with; dealing with mine would have been too much. At least, that's what I had convinced myself of.

Eventually I let my pride down, called my father, and tearfully asked if I could return home. Three weeks later, he was in Nashville helping me move my things back to Chicago. You'd think this was the worst of it all. The end of it all. It wasn't. Nowhere near. I returned to Chicago in 2008, and the only thing comfortable about it was the fact that I had a home to return to. Reality was getting ready to set in. Several realities, actually: the reality of who my friends were and were not, the reality of fighting to get back to normal (whatever the hell that meant), the reality of death, and the reality of people not knowing your worth and treating you as such. I had an ex tell me, in so many words, that he was tired of hearing me cry about my diagnosis all the time, that I needed to get over it because it happened, I didn't die, and should just move on with my life. And although pointing fingers isn't typical of me, I can say with all confidence that his words helped activate a silence and depression in me that lasted 2 years. I suffered through 6 deaths upon my return to Chicago, 3 of which were the family of Oscar/Grammy Award-winning Jennifer Hudson (a childhood friend and vocal partner). A married man supported my lifestyle because I made myself available to him and I needed the money. I was smoking more weed than Snoop Dogg in his twenties. I drank more liquor than your "playa" uncle the night before his wedding. I was fucking so many random men that after a while, I lost count. I was cursing out anyone and everyone who I felt had offended or slighted me in some way. I was crying every day, all day. I was unemployed, broke, and broken......no, shattered. And all because God decided that it was I who needed to have Ovarian Cancer. That I should carry this burden to give someone else with the same burden hope for a better tomorrow. And I hated God, in all forms, for this executive decision made without my knowledge or consent.

I'm going to be as honest and candid as I can, and for two reasons: one, because I don't know any other way to be. Two because I'm a firm believer that truth, while relative, is still truth. And sugar, while it sweetens truth's bitterness, does not negate it. My truth: Ovarian Cancer ruined my entire fucking life. That is a fact. Not to be disputed. Not to be debated. Not to be equivocated. IT RUINED MY ENTIRE LIFE!!!!!!!!!!!!!! I was supposed to be an opera singer. Now, I'm stuck being the motivation for the chick who has a knife to her wrist. I was supposed to replace Maria Callas as the greatest coloratura soprano to exist. Now, I'm stuck trying to talk people out of a depression that I've had since age 15 and have yet to resolve. I was supposed to be an international vocalist. At best, I was supposed to be the best vocal composer or background singer alive. Not even Luther Vandross or Lisa Fisher would have compared to me. Now, I'm stuck nursing people through their pain. Because they assume that I've worked through mine

It sucks. Watching your friends and family marry and have children, while you sit and allow yourself to be fucked by any man whose dick was hard and with no guarantee that you'll conceive, let alone give birth. It sucks. Watching your class mates graduate, get jobs, and earn promotions while you have to beg McDonald's to hire you just to you can eat. It sucks. Watching the ex who stood by you through your cancer diagnosis and treatment be, and create a whole family, with one of several women he cheated on you with while you were being treated. It sucks. Knowing that God didn't give one iota of a shit what I wanted my life to be. My plans didn't matter. My feelings didn't either. They were both fodder to feed God's humungous ego and cater to his Dave

Chapelle esque sense of humor. I can just hear God now, laughing at and talking to me over a Juvenile track: "Awwwwwwwww....... poor little Tink-Tink thought she was gonna be a singer ha? Thought you were gonna be something great ha? Thought you was doing something, ha? You REALLY thought that plan you laid for your life was gonna happen, ha? And you were serious about it too, ha?????? Did all that schooling, ha? Thinking you was gonna be something special, ha???????????"

After about 18 months of this unhealthy cycle, I started thinking. Well, more like after 18 months, and my father pulling me to the side to inform me that I was stronger than I was giving myself credit for. I felt that I wasn't the only one angry about all this shit. I know I'm not the only feeling like something with me isn't right. I know I'm not the only one drinking, smoking, fucking, and crying my anger away about this shit. There has to be a resolution. Something.... anything other than what I was doing. And there was: it was counseling. A lightbulb went off. A fire was ignited. And for the first time in over 2 years, I knew what I needed to do: I needed to become a mental health counselor.

I'm sure that this decision sounds random. Like a decision I made on a whim during a smoke break. Initially, I wasn't sure how to even go about becoming a counselor. My background was not in psychology or clinical mental health. I hadn't even been to a counseling session to know how they should go. I was still severely broke and broken myself, so who the hell was I going to be able to counsel? I didn't know how I was going to reach who I needed to reach, but I knew that my current way of being and doing things was not working. I couldn't run from my pain; it followed me everywhere. I couldn't keep acting as if things, and I, were fine. They were not, and neither was I. In hindsight, I was destroying all the good parts of myself in an attempt to distance myself from the very cancer diagnosis I felt had destroyed my life. Actually, it was never the cancer that bothered me. The cancer I had was outside of my realm of control. The subsequent feelings and emotions post-treatment were not. It wasn't that I couldn't control my feelings or emotions; I just didn't know how. How do you navigate uncharted territory? It's not entirely impossible. It's how everything that wasn't previously revealed became so. The issue with navigating territory unknown is how to find your way back after going too far.

At present, my life is as normal as can be expected. I am now a mental health counselor and a PhD student. I still live in Chicago. I lecture with 2 cancer support organization. I work with and counsel the LGBTQ youth. I still have aspirations of becoming the first woman of color to be an international spokesperson for Ovarian Cancer. And I still struggle with depression, insomnia, severe anxiety, and severely triggering PTSD symptoms. 12 years later, I still grapple with how I feel my life is a failure in some way. I still struggle with how my friends and families have husbands and children, while I struggle to have either. I still struggle with how easily others came into their careers while I'm still trying to find a niche in mine. I still struggle with feeling like my mother birthed me for no reason other than her disbelief in abortion: clearly, in 35 years, I've done nothing with my life for a mother to feel the need to brag about. I mean come on: I graduated from college twice. Big fucking deal. Anybody with discipline, the finances, and strong will power can do that. I didn't become a teenaged mother: big fucking deal. Anyone who's consistent with their birth control and self-respect can, and has, achieved that goal. I have a job: big fucking deal. So does the person who took my order at Checker's a few days ago. Beating Ovarian Cancer didn't, nor does it, make me anyone special; it just makes me another person who didn't die from it.

I never wanted the responsibility of being someone's hope for tomorrow. That's way too much responsibility. Why would someone want to depend on me for their hope? I haven't done shit but live. And survive. Anyone can do that. You can ask any homeless guy on the street how to live and survive. What the fuck's so special about me that I must, or was even chosen by the Divine to, do it? And trust me: had I known that being someone's beacon of hope for life would become this cumbersome, I'd have told whatever Divine being that decided that giving me Ovarian Cancer was a good idea to go sit in the very hell that they created.

I remember hearing from a pastor once that everyone in life has a roadmap for their own lives. And at the end of that roadmap is all your blessings and everything you've ever wanted or dreamed of. In order to get to the other side of the map, there were certain crossroads you'd encounter. And the choice you would have to make is whether or not you were willing to go beyond those crossroads in order to get to your blessings on the other side of the roadmap. Hindsight tells me that had I seen my road map, I'd have said "Hell no: you better find me another map or another fucking route!!!!!!!!!!!! Because if I have to get ovarian cancer and almost die to receive a blessing, I don't want that shit!!!!!! Give it to somebody else."

I'm sure people who have never had cancer will be tempted to give the obligatory "But you made it.... you survived.... that alone is enough to be grateful. "First off, let us stop assuming that I am ungrateful just because I hated my experience with my diagnosis and subsequent treatment. Just because I'm not singing God praises for sparing my life does not mean that I'd rather be dead. Secondly, I have always found it funny how easily people can tell you how to handle something they have never experienced. Chile, you have never had cancer. Watching someone die from it does not count. They are two totally different experiences with two totally different vantage points. So, to those of you who feel the need to tell me, or any cancer survivor something close to this, here's a bit of advice: shut the fuck up!!!! You weren't asked, and you are not in the position to dictate to anyone how to process their experience. Especially if you've never had said experience. And telling me to be grateful for my life doesn't negate my feelings of feeling like Ovarian Cancer destroyed it somehow.

I may not ever get over my diagnosis. I live with the reality that it happened. I have the physical scars as reminders of the experience. I suffer with paralyzing and debilitating issues as a result of it. I live in fear that it will come back and kill me on a daily basis. So I can't ever really get over it. I have just had to learn how to live my life despite it. Have I done that yet: no. But dammit, I'm giving it a good old college try. And I'm okay with that.

AUTHOR BIO

Kawana Williams, M.A., LPC was born in Carbondale, Illinois and raised in Dallas, TX where she began writing poetry and short stories at age 5. Her family relocated permanently to Chicago, Illinois in 1992. Raised on the South Side of Chicago, Williams began professionally performing at age 10 at ETA Creative Arts Theater under the tutelage of Runako Jahi and Geraldine "Mama Geri" Williams. Williams is an alumnus of Proviso West High School, graduating in 2001. Williams was diagnosed with Stage I-C Ovarian Cancer while completing her studies at Fisk, postponing her 2006 graduation; she went on to receive a Bachelor of Music-Vocal Performance in 2007 post-diagnosis/treatment. Williams also graduated from St. Xavier University, graduating with a Master of Art-Community Counseling in May of 2013. Williams was inducted into Sigma Gamma Rho Sorority, Incorporated in December of 2006, and into Chi Sigma Iota

Counseling Academic and Professional Honor Society in 2018. In her spare time, Williams has been a volunteer lecturer with the Chicago branches of Gilda's Club and the National Ovarian Cancer Coalition, respectively. She is currently a Licensed Professional Counselor and doctoral student at The Chicago School of Professional Psychology (Chicago/Grayslake) in Chicago, Illinois.